FOR ANYONE WHO IS, OR SOON WILL BE, OR MIGHT SOMEDAY BE an IN-LAW

written by
Jackie Monsour Smith

illustrated by
Kim Oswalt

WGA registered 2209231 2023

All rights reserved. No part of the book may be used or reproduced in any manner whatsoever without written permission except in the case of brief quotations embodied in critical articles and reviews.
Printed in the United States of America

ISBN: 978-1-7351467-5-1

A JackieMo Book

Special thanks

to
Jessica Hennings,
Cj Taylor,
and Rachel Gillie
for their suggestions and edits

to
Moses Hennings
for his creative caricatures

A tribute to

Myra and Dudley

who light the path
by example
and make it
oh so fun
along the way!

Written with gratitude for

Steve  and his kindred soul

Karisa  and her courageous brain

Spencer  and his humble decency

Mike  and his witty determination

Megan  and her unifying gratitude

Trevor  and his thoughtful growth

Lizzie  and her listening love

Artist: Moses Hennings, 10 years old

THE RULES TO READING
IN

FIRST: This book was inspired by wisdom from my very own mother-in-law, Myra Jaccard Smith, whose actions, words, and compassion made her my second mom. Apply as you will!

SECOND: Each chapter heading is a remedy for life wrapped up in one of Myra's common phrases that became truisms in my life. Take the chapter headings to heart!

THIRD: Each chapter starts with a stereotypical joke and ends with suggestions of what to do (IN) and what not to do (OUT). Use this book to break the stereotype!

FOURTH: Keep in mind, the book is more what you call guidelines than actual rules.

PREFACE

Our oldest child inherited my dark, middle-eastern skin. When she was five years old, she sat in the bathtub and scrubbed her arms with a sponge and soap. We weren't talking about her skin, but she scrubbed harder.

With all the defensiveness five-year-old eyes can muster, she stared me down. "I am white, like Daddy. I do not have ugly, dark skin like you." She continued to scrub as if she were scouring the dirt off a four-wheeler truck.

Sometimes the union between two individuals can generate a feeling that the couple needs to choose between their cultures, values, looks, or traditions, one being "better" than the other. Instead, a healthy balance in a marriage should create a blending of these ideals, valuing both heritages while creating a new legacy.

The over simplified story of a five-year-old girl, perceiving her dark skin as a separation from her father, is a perfect opportunity to teach children to experience, embrace, and learn from every trait unique to their heritage on both sides.

So far, this all sounds pretty obvious. Of course marriage means blending and compromise and acceptance. Good enough. However, why have some of the most difficult connections stemmed from in-law relationships? The answer is simple—it's the clashing of that deep-rooted, immeasurable, protective love of a parent with the fresh, hopeful, promising love of a spouse. Transferring these loves to an entire family takes thoughtful, selfless action that can blossom into a profound new experience.

My intent on writing this book is to help others make in-law relationships satisfying, pleasurable, and enduring.

Chapter 1

WHAT IN THE SAM HILL?

So embarrassed. I was a busty teenager and this dress left no doubt in anyone's mind. Her son was taking me to the homecoming dance. Her arms were folded and her eyes averted. Her lips were tightly pulled in, as if there were something trying to escape from her mouth. It finally did. "Well, they sure don't make dresses like they did in my day."

His father pulled him aside, handed him some cash, then turned to me. "Did you bring a jacket? It's going to get chilly. You should put it on."

Thankfully, this is exactly what my future in-laws did **NOT** do when their son took me to a high school dance. I'm sure that this white, all-american, upstanding, Mormon boy choosing to date a middle-eastern, liberal, agnostic teenager, was enough to leave them thinking, **What in the Sam Hill?** But things didn't go down like that.

In truth, yes, I was a little embarrassed—and yes, I was a busty teenager—and yes, this dress left no doubt in anyone's mind. Also, in truth, I don't remember the details of that night. I do remember how I felt.

I felt welcome. I felt like they were interested in who I was. I felt like they cared about their son.

Every interaction between a parent and a future spouse will affect three things that will have long term impact on the future—

ONE, *how your child chooses their future spouse.*
>Depending on if your child tries to please you, or would rather do anything but please you, if you are quick to judge your child's dates, they may choose someone based on your reactions instead of their own feelings. This will leave them feeling powerless, not only in their relationship with you, but also in their marriage.

TWO, *how your child thinks you feel about their spouse.*
>When a young person is in love, suddenly, their brain doesn't work. Except for the hormones part— that part is working just fine. If you pit yourself against your child in an effort to negate their choice, they tend to unite and make it the two of them against the world. Your child might share your comments with their partner. Those words—your words—even if they are misconstrued, are difficult to ever overcome.

THREE, *how that couple will relate to you as parents.*
>If your child sees you as an ally, they will come to you for advice. If their spouse sees you as supportive, they will share their joys and sorrows with you. The opposite is also true, so it is my goal to share experiences with you that will help you forge trusting, strengthening, peaceful relationships as your family grows through marriages.

Seven years later my big bust and I married that young man, and his family too. My heart was full with the idea of getting new in-laws, but it might not have been like that. I could have dreaded the idea.

As a parent, burning bridges early on leaves a chasm of rubble and ash, making it difficult to cross over from one place to the other. You don't want to be on one side of that bridge and your child on the other, even when your child chooses to date someone that leaves you thinking, **What in the Sam Hill?** Be careful, but always be on the same side of the bridge as your child.

Don't get me wrong, we all make judgments when we meet someone. It's human nature to try to make sense of things. But instead of blaming your child, their partner, or yourself, ask why. Gain knowledge about who your child is rather than who they choose to date. If you feel their choice needs to change, it begins with helping them change how they see themselves, not huffing and puffing about their partner's nose ring, anarchist tattoo, or low cut dress.

Teach them how to make good choices with confidence and then let them make choices. Let them know you trust them.

There is a difference between your child's high school dates and dates as an adult, but keep in mind that every person your child dates is a potential spouse. The ideas discussed here should be applied at different levels, according to the seriousness of the individual situation, but whether the dating is casual or meaningful, building a bridge of trust with your child is key.

*DO take an interest in your child's dates.
*DO learn the name of who they are dating.
(I take great exception to this rule for my husband. He made it a tradition to not remember ANY of the kids' names who our children dated until they were practically engaged. It was humorous, endearing, and consistent. This is an all or nothing rule. Don't play favorites.)
*DO ask the date about their interests.
*DO ask your child what they think about the person they are dating.
*DO ask your child periodically how their partner is doing.
*DO bug your child! Bug them a lot! Ask lots of outlandish, fun questions about their dates and experiences. They will blow you off, but don't stop. Keep bugging them so when they really do need someone to talk to, they choose you because they know you're ready to listen.

*DO NOT criticize the partner—this includes their appearance, their modesty or lack of, their use of language, their talents, their past, and their family.

*DO NOT include them in family gatherings on a regular basis.

*DO NOT prefer them over or compare them to any other person your child chooses to date. You never know who your child might go back to and ultimately choose.

*DO NOT make the partner part of your family before they are engaged. This includes adding them to family chats, including them on group gifts, or sharing very personal family situations. This will make it terribly difficult for your child to break up with someone who is not right for them. They might feel as if they are betraying you. They may question their own judgment and even marry that person based on your desires, not theirs.

INSIDE TIP

Look at the person your child is dating as a ball of string. You do not know what is wrapped up in that ball of a soul that has rolled forward for years accumulating experiences. You have to take time to unravel it string by string.

Instead of quickly judging them as *overbearing*, turn it around by seeing them as *ambitious*. Instead of *people pleaser*, look for *generous*. Instead of *overachiever*, try *accomplished*. Instead of *antisocial*, appreciate their *calm*.

Untie what got them there. Understanding a person will alleviate fear and lead to compassion.

Chapter 2

SHE DIDN'T MEAN IT LIKE THAT

While in college, I stayed in touch with my high school sweetheart. Even while pursuing different interests and dating others, we stayed very close. During my senior year of college, I brought home a boy I had been dating to come and meet my family. After meeting my family, I took this boy right over to meet my high school sweetheart's family. We arrived to find them in an extended family gathering. After a short visit, we left.

I later learned an uncle who was there couldn't believe I would bring a boy over to their home to meet them while I was still in touch with their son. He commended Myra for being such a great lady, but also denounced me for being so presumptuous as to hurt their feelings. Myra's response? "Oh, she didn't mean it like that."

When, ***Oh, she didn't mean it like that,*** can be your first reaction, as Myra's always was, you are shifting yourself from feeling like the victim of something hurtful, to clear the path for a better understanding of any situation. This should roll right off your tongue when anyone makes an accusation about your child-in-law.

Myra's attitude continued into the first years of our marriage. When I got married, I was scared and unprepared. While I was dealing with this brand new marriage and an unexpected baby in that first year, Myra never gave up on me. She was hurt. She knew her son was dealing with my scattered emotions, but instead of huffing and puffing behind my back, she called me. She asked me what I was worried about and what I was struggling with. Then, she asked how she could help. This wasn't because she was happy-go-lucky or things didn't affect her. It was because she chose to listen first.

When I chose not to attend family events, I am sure my in-laws were disappointed, but they extended empathy and never brought it back up to me in later times. When I returned gifts they gave me just to prove they didn't know me well, they withheld judgment.

One day my father-in-law, Dudley, said, "hop in the car. We're going shopping."

I still remember the vest I picked out. Dudley insisted on buying me something I liked. They were both school teachers and of moderate means, but Dudley didn't give me a price limit or ever bring it up again.

Myra and Dudley forgave me if I was having a bad day, or even a bad year. Myra gave me a break, a way out so I didn't feel trapped for making one bad choice. Dudley gave me the benefit of the doubt.

When I finally got my act together, I didn't face any backlash. I faced open arms. As I overcame my struggles, Myra bought gifts for my children, included me in family plans, and went shopping with me. Dudley helped me buy Christmas gifts and listened to me play piano. They both spoke highly of me to other people.

My father-in-law pulled me aside to talk to me about God. He wanted me to know that God assured him I was his daughter and always would be.

*DO listen with empathy.

*DO put yourself in their shoes.

*DO get to know your daughter/son in-law's background.

*DO ask yourself, *where are they coming from?*

*DO ask yourself, *what did they bring into the marriage?*

*DO know your new child is still young and growing and learning.

*DO NOT accuse your child-in-law.

*DO NOT use negative labels, like *crazy* or *controlling* or *spiteful*.

*DO NOT seethe over misguided words.

*DO NOT overly analyze meanings.

*DO NOT attach your own ideas to their actions.

*DO NOT automatically side with your child.

INSIDE TIP

The idea of *She didn't mean it like that* has a very peculiar flip side. Although I suggest you extend this courtesy to your in-laws, don't just expect them to extend it to you. You have to acknowledge when you've hurt someone's feelings even if you didn't mean it like that. This will be further discussed in a later chapter.

Chapter 3

NOW GO AND DO WHAT YOU DARN WELL PLEASE!

Looking for homes? Buying furniture? Having children? Should you get involved in these big decisions your children will be making? I would say, absolutely not, but you know what? You can. Myra's approach works like a charm.

The first little condo my husband and I wanted to buy sat behind an old shopping center, in front of a loud railroad track, and next to a senior trailer park. Prices were skyrocketing in 1988 and we were scrambling around wondering how we'd ever got into the housing market. We spent every dime we had by putting $3000 down on this two bedroom condo on the top floor. The carpet was worn, the paint was old, and the cabinets had a few hinges in need of fixing.

This is the first time Myra took a deep breath and plunged into advice mode. I barely remember what she said because she totally caught me off guard with her first comments. They went something like this—

"Jackie, being your mother-in-law, it would make me so happy if you would let me give you guys a little advice about buying this house."

My ears pointed up. My eyebrows raised. My nose could smell danger. I was ready to cross my arms as a defensive shield when she continued.

"One day you'll understand that moms just have to give their opinion. But, after I give you my opinion, you go and do what you darn well please!"

My entire insides collapsed. I laughed out loud and felt this giant, lifetime sense of relief. I pulled my chair up closer to her and rested my elbows on the table, ready to listen.

The greatest surprise? Myra stuck to her word. She spilled out everything she had from the financial risk of buying an old home to the color we should use to paint the walls. When she was done, she truly did allow us to make our own decisions without any rolling of the eyes or *I told you so's*.

This was not a one time thing, so I need you to memorize the phrase, **Now Go and Do What You Darn Well**

Please! Every single time Myra felt compelled to give us advice, I welcomed it with open ears because she always and I mean always ended with the phrase, ***Now Go and Do What You Darn Well Please!*** I smiled every time.

Let me give you a few examples where this phrase would more than likely strengthen the bond between you and your child-in-law.

PLANNING WEDDINGS

*DO ask the couple about their vision for the wedding.

*DO offer financial alternatives that might be more reasonable for that vision.

*DO offer logistical advice to help carry out the vision, like, *Uncle Tuba's shellfish allergy wouldn't be able to handle shrimp cocktail, how about smoked salmon appetizers?*

*DO let them know about wedding traditions in the family, and then DO let them decide if they want to incorporate those traditions.

*DO say after every piece of advice, *Now Go and Do What You Darn Well Please.*

PLANNING WEDDINGS

*DO NOT worry about what your friends will think of the feathered crowns on the bridesmaids, the fanny packs the groomsmen are wearing, the shoeless bride, or the sockless groom.

*DO NOT suggest colors you think would flow better.

*DO NOT worry so much about the look of the wedding as you do about the look of your relationship.

# INSIDE TIP

My own mother used to say, "It's not about the wedding, it's about the marriage." Always thought that was wise and thoughtful of her.

HAVING BABIES

*Hmmmm I can't think of any DO's, but if you must—

*DO say after every piece of advice, *Now Go and Do What You Darn Well Please.*

HAVING BABIES

*DO NOT advise your children when to have children.
*DO NOT ask them if they're trying to have a baby.
*DO NOT tell them you're going to die a lonely old person without grandkids.
*DO NOT gasp at or try to change any name choices they share.
*DO NOT use nicknames you are asked not to use.

INSIDE TIP

This is for mother/daughter-in-laws—
Don't expect your daughter-in-law's pregnancy to mirror yours. Bodies are different, temperaments are different, hormones are different, care is different. Just because you gave birth in a bathtub in your living room does not mean it's wrong for her to lie in a hospital bed with epidural medication on speed dial.

RAISING CHILDREN

*DO share stories about your child when they were growing up.

*DO ask about your in-laws' childhood and growth.

*DO honor parental restrictions on food and curfews and discipline.

*DO offer helpful tips about breastfeeding, bottles, preparing food, bedtime routines, discipline methods and everything in between that worked for you.

*DO say after every piece of advice, *Now Go and Do What You Darn Well Please.*

RAISING CHILDREN

*DO NOT contradict the parent in front of the grandchild.
*DO NOT feed your grandchild in a different manner than their parent's method. If your child-in-law asks you not to feed your grandchild sugar, DON'T FEED THEM SUGAR. There is no scooping of ice cream on your finger when the parents aren't looking. There is no marshmallow cereal for a snack when you're watching the kids for the day.
*DO NOT talk about the grandchild you see more when you're with the grandchild you see less. Talk about their children, that family, and how stinking awesome they are!

# INSIDE TIP

Do not replace your parenting for grandparenting. Stay fresh and available to your own children as a parent, especially those who are single or do not have children.

Chapter 4

Don't Be a Martyr

This chapter title does not belong to my mother-in-law. It belongs to one of my sister-in-laws.

I'm dedicating this whole chapter to my three sister-in-laws because they have all taught me something about in-laws worth sharing.

Sister-in-law #1: Kind like a sister—

My oldest sister-in-law didn't live near her family when her brother and I started dating, so when we were married, I didn't know her quite as well. When we were expecting our first baby, she sent me a baby gift as a congratulations. I thought that was so sweet and I thanked her.

The next month, I received another gift from her. I thanked her again and said it wasn't necessary to give me a second gift, but very fun.

The third month I received another gift and I was almost embarrassed. I hoped she didn't think I expected her to give me a gift every month of my pregnancy.

What I learned after nine months of very thoughtful gifts from my sister-in-law was that she didn't think I expected it at all, but she treated me like she treated her other sisters. She included me in this family tradition and I was truly overwhelmed. So overwhelmed in fact that we named that first child after her.

Sister-in-law #2: Genuine advice like a sister—

My middle sister-in-law helped me change with helpful, constructive advice. For example, she noticed me slamming cupboards a little loudly one day. She sat me down and said these words that still ring in my ears, "Don't be a martyr."

It was obvious I was mad at my husband and obvious to her that he had no idea why. She didn't criticize me or take her brother's side, but helped make the situation better. She told me to tell my husband what was bothering me rather than expecting him to know. It worked.

Sister-in-law #3: Loyal like a sister—

My youngest sister-in-law was two grades below me. One time, she was standing near me as I stood in a circle of my high school friends. Someone joked about something I had done in the past that wasn't anything I would have wanted to share with her family. I gave her a quick little *Eeek-I'm-sorry-you-had-to-hear-that* glance. She pulled me a bit to the side. I don't remember exactly how she said it, but it was very quick and casual.

"Don't worry about it. I don't care what people say and I'd never say anything to anyone."

That soft comment made me trust her. She held confidences and was always willing to give someone a chance.

Do not misunderstand me—it's taken me a lifetime of working out our differences to learn to be a sister-in-law. However, that journey has been more intentional and thoughtful for me because of all three of their first inclinations to include and accept.

It's human nature to value traits common to your own heritage. I was a petite, dark, round brunette who married into a tall, skinny, blonde family. I didn't dress like they did. I didn't have the same political ideas as they did. I didn't have the same cultural ideals of raising kids as they did. They were very sports driven while I was raised exposed to the arts. The clashing of these values can be painful and flourishing all at the same time.

The flourishing part comes from inclusive behaviors and looking at people from their perspective.

These are the things I've learned, sometimes the easy way and sometimes the hard way, as the IN and OUT of brother/sister-in-lawing.

*DO consider your own sibling and their love for their spouse, your new in-law.

*DO invite your sibling-in-law to participate in family traditions.

*DO give your sibling-in-laws the option of being included in group gifts and family group planning

*DO take lots of sister/brother pics and include everyone.

*DO be open and explicit about your own boundaries when it comes to dropping in or watching one another's children.

*DO NOT tell stories that presume you know your sibling better than your sibling's spouse does. When telling a story about your sibling as a child, instead of saying things like, *you don't know him/her like I do,* end it with, *does he/she still do that?*

*DO NOT gossip or criticize your new sibling's family. Even if they complain about their own family, sympathize greatly, but do not criticize. Your goal is to help them recognize where they can mend their relationship with their own family, not replace them with you.

*DO NOT gossip about your sibling in-laws.

*DO NOT expect your new sibling to dress like your family does. When I wore styles that widened the eyes of my in-laws, there were times I felt ridiculed, but my husband always stepped up and supported my fashion choices which really helped me to not take offense.

*DO NOT ever speak poorly about their children, especially in front of your own children.

*DO NOT ever try to take the place of a parent with one of their children. Your intention of helping a niece or nephew should always be to guide them back to their parents.

*DO NOT share anything they tell you in confidence about their spouse or children.

*DO NOT praise or criticize physical appearances about your children. "I'm so glad her hair turned blonde." Or "I was afraid he might be short, but he finally grew." These are words that should never be spoken, but especially not if your sibling in-law is short or has brown hair.

INSIDE TIP

There will be times when a competitive nature may arise between you and your new siblings, especially after you all have children. My advice is to fight that nature. Do not feel lesser about yourself or your own child as the result of a success of one of your sibling-in-laws or their children. Encourage everyone, including yourself, to cheer on those successes. You will feel better about yourself and your relationships. The way to make your own child feel secure after witnessing the achievements of others is to develop your own child's talent, not to put down another child. Making excuses like, *their parent is on the board* or *they have more money than we do,* will only dampen the way your child views life and their relationship with their cousin.

Chapter 5

GOODNIGHT GENEVIEVE!

The first time I witnessed a Christmas celebration in my husband's home, I was sincerely confused. There is no other way to put it. Who were all these presents for? I wasn't informed that more people were coming. I hadn't been told we would need to clear two days to open presents. I just sat—a bit flabbergasted.

As the morning unfolded, it became clear that no one else was coming and that this Christmas tradition would take, not only all morning, but well into the afternoon as we opened presents one by one.

In contrast, in the household where I grew up, presents just weren't that big of a deal. There was a sweet exchange of gifts and nobody had to watch anybody else open. Food? That was a big deal.

Traditions are ingrained in us so deeply it can be mind boggling when you discover not everyone celebrates holidays like you do.

If you're standing under the mistletoe together, you have to kiss. Right?

The oldest person in the family lights the last candle on the Menorah. Right?

Ram Navami parties are always costume themed. Right?

Baked kebee and dates are a must at the feast ending Ramadan. Right?

Santa always leaves one unwrapped gift under the tree. Right?

WRONG!

But really not right or wrong.

Goodnight Genevieve! This is Myra's way of expressing herself when she can't quite wrap her mind around something. Marrying into family traditions can be jarring, even bewildering. People tend to throw up walls and roadblocks when participation feels expected, instead of invited.

There are two types of traditions. First, there are sacred traditions that are practiced as true worship. Rituals of all faiths and denominations are meant to bring us closer to a higher truth, a God, a sense of peace, or a place of belonging. Traditions can feel like an opposition to those things if they are forced or done begrudgingly. Sacred traditions will be respected and even revered by new members of your family if they are invited to participate with love and then met with patience and understanding if they choose to stay on the sidelines. Anything bringing you closer to a higher power or a deeper relationship takes patience, understanding, and love.

The second type of tradition are those activities you've done for years that have brought so much fun and joy to your family that they almost feel sacred to you, but they are not. The Tooth Fairy. The Easter Bunny. Santa. Trick or Treat. Birthday songs. Family reunions.

Family choirs. Matching Christmas Eve pajamas. Girl's night out. Family dinners. I could fill the rest of the book with these. If you have an in-law who loves to party with you, keep it all going. If not, be flexible and meditate on the real intent of carrying out traditions. Be willing to bend these types of traditions or create new ones based on the personalities that enter your family. Focus your efforts on making your new in-law feel connected, loved, and permanent.

Family traditions create unifying family bonds and are an absolutely beautiful way of expressing our commitment, our unity, our pride, and our devotion to our upbringing and our family, but these **_Goodnight Genevieve_** moments take understanding and compromise from all sides.

These well intended gestures must be handled gently and thoughtfully. The following IN and OUT suggestions are separated for parent-in-laws and child-in-laws.

PARENT-IN-LAW

*DO introduce your traditions to your new in-laws.

*DO respect their decision to decline your invitation to participate.

*DO create or add to traditions based on your child-in-law's hobbies, likes, and habits. When your son-in-law's dog wins your March Madness bracket, celebrate the win. Make it clear that they are a wonderful addition to your family dynamics.

*DO treat your children-in-laws special when buying gifts. If all your daughters get a gift, make sure your daughter-in-law does too. Also, get them things related to THEIR interests, not yours. It's ok to bring a few of your customs to them, but add a twist that helps them know you see them. If your whole family looks good in white and they don't, buy them the cream one! Give them room to breathe.

*DO ask your child-in-law what traditions they keep in their own family.

*DO accept new gestures from them that add to your family traditions.

*DO stay flexible.

PARENT-IN-LAW

*DO NOT expect your new in-law to embrace all of your traditions.
*DO NOT exercise punishments for those who do not participate.
*DO NOT pressure anyone to attend family events. NO guilt. No shaming. No passive manipulation. Just a *come if you can* attitude.
*DO NOT create traditions that are exclusive. For example, when you create traditional activities or gifts for grandchildren, leave room for a couple that doesn't have children. Keep them included and special as well.
*DO NOT roll your eyes or speak poorly of your new in-laws for creating their own boundaries.
*DO NOT EVER pit your child against their spouse in order to get them to participate in old family traditions.

INSIDE TIP

A growing family necessitates change. Traditions that were quiet, small, or cozy might not be feasible when your family doubles in size. Keepsakes, memory books, and oral stories will help you cherish the beautiful memories you created. Treasure those things, but know when it's time to move on.

CHILD-IN-LAW

*DO listen with the intent of understanding the traditions of your new family.

*DO make an effort to participate in the traditions that will unite you with the family.

*DO bring your own style, twist, or culture into their traditions.

*DO express gratitude for the efforts of your in-laws to include you.

*DO create your own traditions with your spouse that do not include anyone else.

*DO stay flexible.

CHILD-IN-LAW

*DO NOT mock the traditions of your new family.

*DO NOT assume anyone knows how you feel about an event. Express your concerns if the tradition is offensive to you.

*DO NOT EVER pit your spouse against their own parents by asking them to choose between you and their family traditions.

*DO NOT create a division by uniting all the in-laws against the family. It's okay to confide in one another for comfort, but don't make it an angry mob.

INSIDE TIP

Instead of getting offended that your new family doesn't see you like you want them to, show them who you are. If you're not an athlete and they do competitive games every memorial day, offer to add a drawing competition or a math trivia to the games. They will come to appreciate who you are as it adds a new flavor to their family dynamics.

Chapter 6

Have you ever wanted to say, **Golly Moses!**?

No? Never? How about when your mother-in-law tells you a story about your husband as a fifth grader jumping into a county wide cross country meet and beating the top runners in Orange County by a long shot while wearing basketball shoes? Or maybe when she brags about him running punts and kick off returns for more touchdowns than any other scorer in Jr All American football? Or possibly when she gloats that he was the recognized star of the little league all star team? Or when she reminds you all the older kids on the street would pick him first for the neighborhood games? Or when she boasts about how he won the county highjump every year?

    You think I'm done, don't you? But she isn't—she continues for thirty years about how he was moved up to the varsity volleyball team as a freshman and how he was either Captain or MVP in every sport he played and how he entered the boys club to play basketball and jumped into a ping pong tournament and won the whole thing and how he was offered several volleyball scholarships including one to Stanford, but played for UCLA instead. And then she says, "Golly Moses! He is such an athlete!"

Maybe you'd like to respond by saying, "Oh, please, not again!" or "Seriously? He doesn't walk on water!" But if you learn to say, **Golly Moses!** or whatever form you use for *that's awesome*, you've opened up bragging rights and that can be so much fun!

Let your parent-in-law brag about their child. Agree with them! Ironically, when you let your in-laws know you agree that your spouse is pretty amazing, they will become impartial when a situation arises where they are helping you settle an argument or make a decision. They will relax their need to prove the worth of their child.

Seem counter intuitive? Let me explain—

When your in-laws understand that you respect and admire their child, there will be no need for them to prove their child is perfect, because you will both agree they are not perfect. Your in-laws will see you both as working together and it will be easier to navigate difficult situations.

There is something in a parent that springs from the depths of the universe causing them to defend their child beyond logic because, if a parent won't, who will?

You can help parents overcome the tendency to always side with their child by letting them tell the world, or at least you, how incredible their child is. Once they understand that you know their child is intelligent, brave, athletic, creative, loyal, compassionate, or whatever it is they want you to know, it leaves room for the parent to think maybe you are right and possibly their child is wrong when there is an argument to be discussed.

It's amazingly comforting to a parent when they've spent years defending their child to the world that someone can share that child's **Golly Moses** moments with them and believe every word.

My in-laws know that my husband is stubborn. They know he tends to argue until he's right. They also know that I know he's all sorts of wonderful things. They don't always side with him. Sometimes they side with me and who better to sympathize with you about your spouse's flaws than the other people who love him/her more than life? This worked so well for me that the following incident actually took place. Word for word.

"I'm so mad at you! I'm going to your mom's right now!" Door slams.

Door opens. "*My* mom's? What if *I* want someone to talk to?"

"Go talk to your sister!"

Door slams again.

And I drove to my mother-in-law's and complained to her.

Her reaction? "Good Night Genevieve!"

*DO listen with interest when your spouse's family shares details about them.

*DO ask questions about that history.

*DO take time to look at pictures your in-laws want to show you.

*DO give your in-laws credit for some of the amazing talents your children have.

*DO NOT try to one up their stories with stories of your own.

*DO NOT complain that your spouse is not capable of those things anymore.

*DO NOT remind your in-laws that the last time they told that story their child made the winning basket with five seconds left on the clock—not three.

INSIDE TIP

One of the greatest things about letting your in-laws brag about their child to you is the circle it creates when you have children of your own. You will have the biggest listening ears around when it's time to brag about your own children.

How many mother-in-laws does it take to change a light bulb?

One. She just holds it and waits for the world to revolve around her.

Chapter 7

But Fox News Said

Politics? Shhhhh. Are we actually going to talk about politics? Close the door. Make sure the kids are in the other room and please turn off Alexa so I don't get any campaign ads on my feed.

Discussing politics and social issues has become more and more combative over the years, but it has always been a source of opposition. As a young married person I was caught off guard at how opposing those thoughts could be when I heard my in-laws discuss politics.

My ideologies and social philosophies came from a very different place than my mother-in-law's. She came from ancestors she could trace back to the Boston tea party. She was born into generations of people who built this country. I was born to parents who were raised in small east coast immigration towns. My father was first-generation born American.

When I married into this family, I was on the defense. I was surprised by the thoughts that didn't align with my ideals. My first instinct was to label these thoughts as bigoted, even ignorant. My feelings didn't go unnoticed.

One day I had a conversation with Myra. I will never forget it. We talked about racial inequality. Her ideas were not what I had imagined. She just thought differently about how the issue should be solved. She gave me examples of what she thought should be done. I told her why I didn't think her ideas would work, so she asked me what my ideas were. By the end of that conversation she said, "you've really helped me think differently about that." The crazy thing was, I didn't walk away gloating that my thoughts prevailed over hers, I walked away feeling closer to Myra than ever before. I walked away with the new found principle of listening when we spoke about politics or anything else we might not agree on. I walked away feeling heard.

Solving the problem is not as easy as I make it sound with the above scenario. I'm not just talking about politics here—so what do you do when you completely disagree with your in-laws?

It starts way before your children choose to get married. Prepare yourself by making a home that encourages respect, curiosity, and confidence.

As much as we try to create a well-balanced home, sometimes the home can become an echo chamber of thoughts. This will not prepare us to welcome new thoughts from in-laws entering in and bursting the family bubble. Inviting varying thoughts is not an easy or comfortable thing to do, especially in our politically polarized world, but it is absolutely necessary for effective communication and true progress.

Some of us will marry into families who have not prepared homes like this. Some of us will gain children-in-laws who have not been raised like this. Some of us are just not prepared ourselves. There is no painless fix to this problem, but if you jump in with an open mind, a willingness to listen, and a commitment to swallow some pride, you will slowly notice your example changing hearts.

When it comes time for you to speak, don't be afraid to let your in-laws know that you don't agree with them. Do it with respect and an openness to an alternate way of thinking.

I'm not going to pretend that there weren't moments when my in-laws didn't throw their hands up and wonder how on earth I could think the way I think. The point is, they allowed me to think and that in turn helped me to allow them the same.

*DO allow your in-laws to have different thoughts than you.

*DO acknowledge that you understood, not just heard, what they are saying before springing into your own thoughts.

*DO keep your mind open to new ways of thinking.

*DO understand that there is more than one way of looking at an issue.

*DO keep yourself humble enough to admit when you are wrong.

*DO try to understand what circumstances in your in-laws' life would lead them to these new thoughts.

*DO make yourself heard. Be sure to explain that you do not feel the way they do about a particular issue. Ask them if they would let you explain.

*DO invite group discussions into your home on seminars, podcasts, and articles that are based on the opposite of your opinion.

*DO allow your own child to grow and learn new things from their spouse. They may be exposed to things you didn't teach in the household and those things may resonate more soundly for them right now.

*DO understand that some of the things you taught will come creeping back to them as they raise their own children.

*DO NOT interrupt your in-law when they are speaking.
*DO NOT assume you know what they are thinking.
*DO NOT ask for donations or support on an issue on which you know they are strongly opposed.
*DO NOT make every family gathering about politics
*DO NOT assume your child will marry someone who has the same values, thoughts, and stances that you do. Give your children-in-laws and your children the space to grow together and make a union that is best for them.

 SIDE TIP

Try at times to support or praise an in-law for something they are involved in or have accomplished that doesn't align with your values at all. It's inspiring, uplifting, and down right refreshing.

Chapter 8

I googled Wowdee Dowdee, but I couldn't find it anywhere. Actually, I found one comment that says it has no clear origin or meaning. I'm convinced it was slang for *so cool* in the 1940s. Wherever it comes from, I can assure you it's a word—also, it's quite the magical word. It's a word Myra uses.

I've definitely saved the best part for last. I mean, who doesn't want a **Wowdee Dowdee** in their life?

This last chapter will give you the WOW factor of any in-law relationship. The WOW factor—are you ready for it? It's the secret to relationships that humans have been searching for since the beginning of time. It's all about the magic word. You'll be amazed. Are you ready?

The magic word? Did you think I meant please? Not even close.

The magic word is, has been, and always will be **sorry**. Sorry possesses all the magical depth of Harry Potter.

I myself have been the perpetrator of many of the things I've advised you not to do. We all make mistakes. A genuine *I'm sorry* is healing, enduring, and unifying.

I apologize when I've misjudged or misstepped or misspoken. Never slipping up or making mistakes is not an option for any of us—we are all human. Having that five letter word up your sleeve for just such occasions is effective, calming, even life-altering.

*DO keep your apologies sincere.

*DO make your apologies in person, by phone, by card, by email, by text. Choose a way which makes you both comfortable.

*DO make apologies for things you did as a parent. I like to apologize for things like shopping for my kid's clothes and returning what they didn't like and rebuying until they did like it. Not a great idea for humans who eventually need to shop for their own clothes.

*DO try things that are a little out of your comfort zone. Give hugs. Make cookies. Look at your person in the eye. Have a good cry with them. This will create bonds.

*DO NOT blame someone else for your mistake.
*DO NOT promise you will never ever ever make a mistake again.
*DO NOT pretend the mistake never happened.
*DO NOT beat yourself up when you mess up—this is the most important step. DO NOT forget, you're a good human being!

INSIDE TIP

When your son/daughter in-law apologizes to you for something like not making their bed that morning when you happen to be there, respond with "I didn't make my bed for an entire year, so no judging here." Make sure your response is true like I did, but when your in-law apologizes to you for something that doesn't matter, make sure they understand you are not judging them and that you completely understand.

Conclusion

 I used to think Myra and Dudley were special and unique because they were just born that way. Now I realize, there really are people who are happy, not because of their genetic make-up, but because they create happiness. It doesn't mean they never experience anything difficult. It doesn't mean they don't learn or change as they grow through life. It just means they choose and I mean really choose to see the good.

To see the light. To see the better. I watched Myra and Dudley do that.

If you choose to look at things from a different perspective, to use your trials to help you grow and build relationships, I promise you a good IN with your in-laws.

*Intreat me not to leave thee,
or to return from following after thee:
for whither thou goest, I will go;
and where thou lodgest, I will lodge:
thy people shall be my people,
and thy God my God.*
Ruth 1:16

www.ingramcontent.com/pod-product-compliance
Lightning Source LLC
Chambersburg PA
CBHW061401160426
42811CB00100B/1371